Mighty Matty and Super Seb

by Catherine Casey
illustrated by Pauline Gregory

Matty and Seb liked to see films and read comics. They liked reading about characters with superpowers.

Some of them could …

“I wish I had superpowers,” said Matty.

“Me, too,” said Seb.

It was time to go to school. Dad picked up the car keys.

“We could go on our bikes,” said Seb.

"Bikes are better for the planet," replied Matty.

"It is great for fitness, too," said Seb.

"Sure, we can go on our bikes," agreed Dad.

So Dad, Matty and Seb went on their bikes. They all had helmets and reflective tops on.

"This feels great," smiled Dad.

After school, Dad was watering the garden.

“You could use the rain water we collected,” Matty advised.

“Oh, it is quicker this way,” complained Dad.

"We can help you save water," said Seb.

Matty and Seb filled up the watering cans. They watered the plants.

“Time to go food shopping,” said Dad.

“Let’s take these reusable bags,” said Matty.

“Single-use bags are really bad for the planet,” said Seb.

At home, Dad started to put the shopping away. There were lots of boxes and plastic. It made lots of rubbish.

Matty and Seb were reading their comic books. Some characters were flying between the clouds. They used their powers to save people.

"I wish I had superpowers," said Matty again.

"Me, too. What could our superpowers be?" said Seb.

Dad gave them a smoothie made with blackberries they had picked.

"Yummy, and blackberries picked locally, too," said Matty.

"Made for my two planet-saving superstars," said Dad.

Seb and Matty took their empty glasses into the kitchen.

"Wow, there is so much rubbish, Dad," said Seb.

"We can recycle some of this," said Matty.

Matty and Seb were good at recycling. They sorted the paper, plastic and boxes into piles.

Then Seb had a plan.

“We can use the boxes and paper,” explained Seb.

They made capes, masks and big letters for their shirts.

“Meet Mighty Matty and Super Seb!” said Seb. “Our superpowers are protecting the planet.”

Back at school, it rained hard at breaktime. Seb's coat was way too small now. It was a good job they had to stay inside.

Then Super Seb had an idea.

“We can organise a clothes swap and reuse things,” he said.

That breaktime, the teacher helped plan a clothes swap.

In the afternoon, Mighty Matty had sports.

"My trainers are too small. They will need to go in the bin," said her friend.

"Not now we have the clothes swap," grinned Mighty Matty.

Posters were put up around the school that day. The clothes swap would happen on Friday afternoon.

The next day, Mighty Matty and Super Seb had fun. They saw everyone reusing things they did not need any more.

“Great job!” said Matty, beaming with pride.

Mighty Matty's and Super Seb's superpower is saving the planet. You can help save the planet, too!

- ☆ Turn off the lights when you leave a room.
- ☆ Turn off the taps when you clean your teeth.
- ☆ Reuse bags for shopping.
- ☆ Put your used paper in the recycling.

Encourage students to talk about the planet-saving tips. Do they think they are good ideas? Do they have any other ideas for saving the planet?